Metaphysics

UNI SLOVAKIA series
Volume 14

Metaphysics
Selected Problems of Metaphysics
and Ontology

Renáta Kišoňová

Bibliographic Information published by the Deutsche Nationalbibliothek

The Deutsche Nationalbibliothek lists this publication in the Deutsche Nationalbibliografie; detailed bibliographic data is available in the internet at http://dnb.d-nb.de

The publication of this book is part of the project Support for Improving the Quality of Trnava University (ITMS code 26110230092) — preparation of a Liberal Arts study program, which was supported by the European Union via its European Social Fund and by the Slovak Ministry of Education within the Operating Program Education. The text was prepared at the Department of Philosophy, Faculty of Philosophy, Trnava University in Trnava.

Design and Layout: © Jana Sapáková, Layout JS.
Printing: VEDA, Publishing House of the Slovak Academy of Sciences

ISSN 2366-2697
ISBN 978-3-631-67368-3
E-ISBN 978-3-653-06622-7
DOI 10.3726/978-3-653-06622-7

© Peter Lang GmbH
Internationaler Verlag der Wissenschaften
Frankfurt am Main 2016

All rights reserved.

Peter Lang Edition is an Imprint of Peter Lang GmbH.
Peter Lang – Frankfurt am Main · Bern · Bruxelles · New York · Oxford · Warszawa · Wien

All parts of this publication are protected by copyright. Any utilisation outside the strict limits of the copyright law, without the permission of the publisher, is forbidden and liable to prosecution. This applies in particular to reproductions, translations, microfilming, and storage and processing in electronic retrieval systems.

This publication has been peer reviewed.

Printed in Slovakia

www.peterlang.com

Contents

1. Introduction 7
2. Clarification of Terms 9
   2.1. Metaphysics 9
   2.2. Being as a Term 10
   2.3. Ontology 12
   2.4. Existence 14
3. Metaphysics and Ontology of Archaic Nations 19
4. Being as The One. Parmenides 25
5. Time and Events in the Greeks. Pre-Socratic Philosophers and Plato 29
6. Metaphysics as a Categorical Description 37
   6.1. Aristotelian Categories 38
   6.2. Kant's Categories 39
   6.3. More Recent Reflections 42
7. Criticism of Metaphysics 45
   7.1. Metaphysics and Postmodernism 48

8.	Metaphysics as a Way to God	51
	8.1. Negative Theology of Dionysius the Areopagite	51
	8.2. Theocentrism of J.S. Eriugena	61
	8.3. Ontological Proof of God according to Anselm of Canterbury	62
	8.4. Five Ways to God of Thomas Aquinas	64
9.	Problems of the Universals	67
10.	Metaphysics and Problem of Intuition. Henri Bergson	71
	10.1. Duration	74
	10.2. Ontology of the Past	80
11.	Metaphysics and Problem of Being. Martin Heidegger	83
	11.1. The Meaning of Being	83
	11.2. "Phenomenon" as an Expression	85
	11.3. "Logos" as an Expression	87
	11.4. Phenomenology	87
	11.5. Fundamental Ontology	90
	11.6. Problem of Metaphysics after the "Turn"	96
Conclusion		101
Bibliography		103

1. Introduction

The presented text offers a basic overview of the terms and topics of the very wide philosophical discipline called metaphysics. Questions and the consequent answers, which are connected with metaphysics, are of several kinds and they are extraordinarily well elaborated in the history of philosophy. It is not possible to mention all of them in a text of this kind and it is also not possible to provide a deep analysis of all the individual topics. After all, to cover the metaphysics of Thomas Aquinas would deserve a text the length of this entire text. However, I believe that this text will help students of philosophy and of pedagogy who teach this kind of topic. The text includes, besides the overview of individual problems, reflections to consider and recommended literature. The reader will become familiar with the basic terms (metaphysics, ontology, existence, being), with the metaphysics of archaic nations because this topic is represented to only a small degree in the themes of classical textbooks of metaphysics and ontology and therefore close attention will be paid to it. Another topic is Parmenides's approach to understanding of being as The One. This theme smoothly turns into another one: the understanding of time and events of the Greeks. Further, the problem of categories according to Aristotle, Kant, and the modern approaches are dealt with. Then follows the topic concerning the criticism of metaphysics, which was opened by Kant. The reader will be then acquainted with the traditional metaphysical question of the approach to God in the conceptions of Dionysius the Areopagite, J.S. Eriugena, Anselm of Canterbury, and Thomas Aquinas. Two large topics of metaphysics with two important authors follow – Bergson and Heidegger whose approaches differ in many respects but both of them are so significant that we dared to dedicate a deeper analysis to them.

I appreciate the discussions which I have been able to hold with students in the course of my lecturing on the subject Ontology at the Faculty of Arts of Trnava University in Trnava. Several reflections for consideration, which can be found in this book, resulted from discussions during lectures.

2. Clarification of Terms

2.1. Metaphysics

It is not easy to define metaphysics. Its importance, method, and subject have been changed quite often in history. It was delimited to science, theology, and later within philosophy, to non-metaphysical philosophical conceptions. The term metaphysics is of Greek origin (ta meta, ta fysika, that which is beyond physics) This term was first documented in the works of the Peripatetic Nicholas of Damascus (born probably in 64 AD), who was probably inspired by another Peripatetic – Andronicus of Rhodes (also born around approximately 60 AD). Andronicus put Aristotle's works in order according to subject where works about "the first philosophy" were put "meta" i.e. "behind" the works about nature (Gr. physis). Aristotle did not know the term metaphysics and he classified the problems, which were later categorised by western philosophy as metaphysics, as "the first philosophy," "wisdom," or "theological science" (Schmidinger, Metaphysic: Ein Grundkurs, 2010).

For Aristotle, metaphysics is a science, which deals with the knowledge of:

1. being as a being
2. principles and causes
3. the highest existence (The First Mover) and his relationship to the world

According to Aristotle's definition, metaphysics is:
"There is a science which investigates being as being and the attributes which belong to this in virtue of its own nature. Now this is not the same as any of the so-called special sciences; for none of these others treats universally of being as being. They cut off a part of being and investigate the attribute of this part; this is what the mathematical sciences for instance do. Now since we are seeking the first principles and the highest causes, clearly there must be something to which these belong in virtue of its own nature" (Aristotle, Metaphysics, 1978).

2.2. "Being" as a Term

Aristotle's definition includes the term "being" which does not belong to the ordinary vocabulary. It is therefore necessary to mention it briefly. According to Aristotle, being is the most general thing about which it is possible to say that it "is." Beings are things and the relations between them, plants, animals, people, inanimate nature but also imagination, ideas, memories, moods. Being is a transcendental term, which means, that which can be categorised for every item that exists. It is therefore everything that exists in some way. Latin uses the term *ens*, Czech *jsoucno*, Greek *eon*, German *das Seiende*, French *l'etant*, as being.

1. Being is possible only on the basis of an ontological difference from nothingness (it differs from the nothingness "only" because it exists).
2. It is the most general term.
3. It cannot be identified with existence: there is an ontological difference between being and existence.

Plato perceived metaphysics as "epopteia" (from the Greek perception, understanding) or, in another way, the reception of the perfect simple and still phenomena (Schmidinger, 2010). These phenomena are, according to Plato, the most basic teachings and the deepest causes of reality which relate to the highest ideas of good and beauty.

Metaphysics changed into a science about God in the Middle Ages. We can find the following definition in the work of Thomas Aquinas: *"Further, knowledge can be concerned only with being, for nothing can be known, save what is true; and all that is, is true. But everything that is, is treated of in philosophical science---even God Himself; so that there is a part of philosophy called theology, or the divine science, as Aristotle has proved"* (Summa Theologica. I,1,1).

In modern times a new term "ontology" emerges alongside the already known term metaphysics.

2.3. Ontology as a Term

As for etymology, the term ontology originated from the Greek word on (to be) or more precisely from the present participle of the word ontos and logos. The term ontology was introduced to philosophy by a German protestant scholar Rudolf Göckel (Rudolphus Goclenius) in his Philosophical lexicon (1613) and it was used in parallel with the terms ontosophia philosophia entis (See e.g.: Walsh, M.J.: A history of Philosophy. London, 1985, p. 557).

In 1661, Duhamel defined ontology as teachings different from natural theology. Ontology was at that time considered to be *"...teachings about the existence of finite beings and of all that fundamentally and naturally belongs to them"* (Walsch, p. 557). Ontology was thus defined as philosophical teachings about being. Even Aristotle and the scholastics identified ontology with metaphysics or with the first philosophy. At the time when ontology began to take off as an individual philosophical discipline, it was closely connected with philosophical teachings about God, with theodicy.

The systematic borderline of ontology can be found in the works of Ch. Wolff's *Ontology*. Wolff distinguishes:

1. *metaphysica generalis* (general metaphysics) – deals with existence and being itself
2. *metaphysica specialis* (special metaphysics)
   - a. rational cosmology (the world itself is a matter of concern)
   - b. rational psychology (the soul is a matter of concern)
   - c. rational theology (God is a matter of concern)

Only Kant's philosophy with "Copernican Turn" radically establishes the question of the possibility of human knowledge and omits ontology from the horizon of possibilities of philosophical knowledge since the terms "existence" and "substance" and the like are not of the most original determination of being but they are a prior categories of reason which occur before each experience.

Another "novelty" of the modern times is a gradual problematisation of the legitimacy of metaphysics. After Kant, the concept of metaphysics was *"...changing into a complex of everything that is problematic, suspicious and reactionary"* (Schmidinger, 2010).

2.4. Existence as a Term

Most metaphysical concepts consider being to be the base of everything in opposition to nonexistence or nothingness. Existence is sometimes simply understood as a synonym for existing (not in the case of the meaning of the Greek term for existence, *einaî*), but in the broad sense, it is connected with existing as such and the term existence is used rather in connection with particular things (The Routledge Companion to Metaphysics, p. 579). Existence relates also to potential or virtual beings. For example Heidegger delimits, when analysing the term existence, three prejudices which are connected across the entire history of the understanding of this term:

1. "existence" is the most general term. But the generality of being does not mean that it is the most evident term and therefore it is not necessary to deal with it any longer. *"The term existence is rather the darkest one"* (Heidegger, 2010).
2. Existence is an undefinable term. This prejudice was rightfully derived from the highest generality of existence. Existence cannot really be expressed and defined as being. *"Existence cannot be definitely derived from higher terms and it cannot be demonstrated by means of the lower ones"* (Heidegger, 2010).

From the above mentioned it is not possible, according to Heidegger, to conclude that existence does not represent a problem. It follows only one determinative moment: existence is not being.

1. Existence is a matter-of-course term. After all, the term existence is used in each utterance, in each relation to being, it is understandable even without further elaboration (see Heidegger, M.: Being and Time, p. 19).

We understand the statement sky *is* blue, I *am* at home, etc. without any problem. It is a case of "an average understandability" which shows non-understandability. It indicates that there is a certain vagueness in each relation to being. *"The fact that we already live with a certain understanding of existence and that the meaning of existence remains shrouded in darkness is proved by the fundamental necessity for the restoration of the question about the meaning of "existence""* (Heidegger, 2010).

As Kahn says, Aristotle distinguishes four important meanings of the Greek term "to be," "einai" in *Metaphysics:*

1. "per accidens" existence: accidental predication
2. "per se" existence: predication according to categories, existence has as many meanings as there are categories
3. "is true;" "is untrue"
4. "be in possibility;" "be in topicality" (see Kahn, CH.H.: The Verb Be in Ancient Greek, 1973)

The Greek *einai* carries an even more fundamental meaning as "only" to exist. If it is used without a predicate it means rather "to be this and that way" or "to be true" (Kahn, 1973). *"To be true is not the same as "to be this way and that way." What is true and untrue is usually a statement created from words: what should or should not be this and that way is a fact or situation in the world"* (Kahn, 1973).

Two aspects belonging to the Greek term "einai" are closely connected with Greek ontology. The first one, which is suggested by Kahn, is **durative**. While most of the verbs in Greek have two or three stems, einai has neither aorist nor perfect and all the tenses of this verb are formed from one present – durative stem (see Kahn, 1973). According to Kahn's analysis, it follows that existence for the Greeks meant something eternal (stable, present), in an undisturbed state of duration. Greek einai cannot simply be translated into the Latin existere. *"Existere etymologically refers to protruding, projecting, to the fact that something is entering existence, emerges from dark background and enters daylight. In addition, this imagination is emphasized by the linguistic structure of the verb because the prefix ex – includes the completion of the process ... existentia ... a state is reached as a result of the emerging process"* (Kahn, 1973).

The second aspect of the Greek einai is the **locative** aspect. Einai is used in the sense of "to be somewhere." Existence has to be in some space, in some place: *"...anything that is, is somewhere, that is nowhere, is not nothing"* (Plato: Gorgias B 3,70).

Reflections to think about:

Try to think over the difference between metaphysics and ontology. Is metaphysics, in your opinion, still a legitimate part of philosophy? What topics used to belong and still belong to the area of metaphysics? Where do the borders of metaphysics end? How would you explain the terms being and existence?

Recommended literature:

http://plato.stanford.edu/entries/metaphysics/
Loux, M.: Metaphysics: A Contemporary Introduction, Routledge, 2013, pp. 1-20.
The Routledge Companion to Metaphysics: 3-7, 578-599

3. Metaphysics and Ontology of Archaic Nations

The historical images of an archaic man result from one ontological concept: being really exists as long as it imitates or repeats an archetype. Everything that is not included in this formula is deprived of meaning and does not have real existence. People from traditional cultures are considered to be real when they, in a certain sense, stop being themselves and participate in the imitation and repetition of what has been preserved by tradition and therefore they should try hard to become archetypal and paradigmatic (see: Eliade, M.: Mýtus o věčném návratu. Praha: OIKOYMENH, 2009, p. 36). Eliade compares archaic ontology with Plato's idea of the passage of history.

A deeper analysis of archetypality and paradigmacity enforcement, the imitation and repetition of the traditions of many years can allow us to understand that an archaic man tolerates history with difficulty; he even tries to cover and eliminate it. His collective memory is *ahistorical* – it stores personalities and stories which become archetypes so they are stored without any exceptional personalities. Archaic society defended itself in various ways against anything new involving history (see e.g.: Sandywell, B.: The Beginnings of European Theorizing – reflexivity in the Archaic Age, Psychology Press, 1996).

All the concepts of "primitive" societies included an idea of the beginning and end of a certain time period which results from the observation and experience of the biocosmological rhythm. A system of periodic purification is a part of these concepts – catharsis, regeneration of life, fasting, and the like. The need for periodic renewal is, with regard to the understanding of history, of particular relevance – it assumes (more or less explicitly) new creation, which means, cyclic regeneration of time from which the "elimination of history" results. The length of a year of individual nations or the lack of stability of the beginning of a new one does not matter (e.g. South African tribe of Yoruba people divide a year into a drought season and a rainy season while their week consists of five days. The months of the Burundian Barundi are based on the cycle of lunar phases which means that their year has approximately thirteen months. The Ghanaian Ashanti divide a month into two periods, each lasting approximately ten days) (see: Eliade, p. 49).

However, periodic rites imply a united idea of "the elimination of history," there are important differences between them – at least as it is a case that there are two ways of understanding history – *historical* and *ahistorical* nations, which are in the literature also described as *civilised* and *primitive*. Historical nations lean towards the idea of a New Year, a repetition of the creation. It is mainly the case for nations which emerged at the outset of history – the Babylonians, the Egyptians, the Jews, and the Iranians. "Primitive" nations perceive time biologically *"...without it being allowed to become „history" that is, without its corrosive action being able to exert itself upon consciousness by revealing the irreversibility of events these primitive societies regenerate themselves periodically through expulsion of „evils" and confession of sins"* (Eliade, p. 67).

The existence of a human is understood in the archaic concepts as a *fall*; the memory of personal experience, historical memory is unbearable. A primitive man feels an unceasing need to free himself from individual memories (mostly sins) history is a collection of them. The regeneration and beginning of a new era starts in primitive societies with a new government, a wedding, the birth of a child – the evil and sins of the past are eliminated and the society heads to a return to the constant *in illo tempore*. For example, the Fijians repeat the act of creation every time yields are low, every time then their existence is in danger and the cosmos seems to be empty, they feel a need to return *in principium*, they expect that the *"...regeneration of cosmic life not from its restoration but from its recreation"* (Eliade, p. 72).

This is the reason why emphasis in the rites is put on the primary, inception, and origin.

A "lunar perspective" dominated in the cosmological-mythological concepts of the Greeks which means that the lunar rhythm together with short intervals (day, week, month, season) functions analogously for longer periods of time – birth of a nation, its development, wearing out, and consequent end. The analogy with the lunar rhythm has an optimistic perspective: as the Moon does not disappear for good, the disappearance of mankind is also not final (after floods, fires, and the like).

From the lunar perspective, although the universe is eternal, it is periodically destroyed by floods or space fire (ekpyrósis). The idea of the destruction of the universe by fire was probably also adopted by Heraclitus. It is even more explicitly present in Zeno and the stoics (see: Eliade, p. 77). Heraclitus' "panta rei" means that everything that passes is elusive and will end. Time and movement for the Greeks are mainly cathagenesis. To become something, to get old, to pass, it all has a pessimistic tone, as the way to death. It is decline marked by a negative sign.

All cosmic-lunar concepts include "the eternal return." Here we encounter a notion of time which is regenerated with each new birth. According to Eliade, this eternal return proves ontology without the intervention of time. "The same way as the Greeks in the myth about the eternal return satisfied their metaphysical desire for "ontic" and static... so does a "primitive" reverse the irreversibility of time by assigning it a cyclical course" (Eliade, p. 78).

All events begin in each moment again and again from the beginning. "The past is only a prefiguration of the future" (Eliade, p. 79). In a certain sense, nothing new is happening in the outer space, everything is only a repetition of the primary archetypal events. The function of time is to allow beings to exist, or more precisely, to appear. But it does not fundamentally influence their existence since it is constantly and periodically regenerating itself (see: Lemon, M.C.: Philosophy of History, London: Routledge, 2003, p 30-33). The Greeks had no idea of any form of creative development in history, their universe is a finite outer space which does not change.

Besides cyclical movements, they paid attention to movements of decline, cathagenesis. According to Aristotle, for example, "*...each change is, by definition, disintegrative. Everything arises and vanishes in time...time itself is rather a cause of disintegration than arising...because change is itself disintegrative*" (Aristotle: Physics. Praha: Rezek, 2010, 4, 222b). And he continues: "*...time consumes everything, wears it out, everything gets old as time passes by...because time itself is rather a cause of disintegration, fthora, because it is number of movements and movement destroys what exists*" (Aristotle, 222a).

Reflections to think about:

Try to characterise the ontology of archaic nations and the Greek understanding of time. How is it different from the understanding of time in the Middle Ages and later in modern times?

Recommended literature:

Lemon, M.C.: *Philosophy of History,* London: Routledge, 2003.
Sandywell, B.: The Beginnings of European Theorizing – reflexivity in the Archaic Age, Psychology Press, 1996.

4. Being as The One. Parmenides

Without exaggeration it is possible to say that Parmenides laid, by means of his philosophical poem, the foundations for ontology as well as for anti-metaphysical positions. He is considered to be the most revolutionary and at the same time the most difficult to interpret of the pre-Socratic philosophers. According to Diogenes Laertius, he wrote only one work, a metaphysical-cosmological poem in hexametre which originally consisted of approximately 800 verses but fewer than 160 of them were preserved.

Reflections on the three ways by means of which we can (or cannot) get to know can be found in Parmenides' fractions. The first way of thinking is the one which says that "something is." Parmenides considers this way to be the right one. Another two ways which say that "nothing is not" and "something is and is not at the same time" are excluded by him: *"I want to tell you – listen carefully to my words and keep them – which ways of examination are the conceivable ones: one that is and cannot be, that is the way of conviction because it follows the truth; the second one that is also not and necessarily does not have to be"* 28 B2 (Antológia z diel filozofov (Predsokratovci Platón, zv.1), p. 118).

"It is necessary to speak and think that existing as being is but nothing is not. I command you to think about it. First, I want to divert you from this way but also then from that way where not knowing two-headed people are writhing; because helplessness in chest leads their helpless mind. But they are rushing, both deaf and blind, lunatics, uncritical crowds which consider existence and non-existence to be the same and not the same for those who have the way back in everything" DK 28 B6 (Antológia z diel filozofov (Predsokratovci Platón, zv.1), p. 118). Parmenides is a an ideal monist. According to him, there is only one being (Eon) and the entire plurality, variability, and difference of beings is only an illusion (doxa). The Eon is characterised as **unborn** (agenéton), **imperishable** (anóletheron), **whole**, **united** (monogenes), **unchanging** (atremes), and **perfect** (teleion). He does not talk about existence (the einai) but about being which later becomes the subject of Heidegger's criticism of Parmenides' understanding of existence as being. Existence is mentioned in his most often interpreted statement: "... for thinking (*noein*) and existence (*einai*) is (*estin*) the same (*to...auto*)" DK 28B3 (Antológia z diel filozofov (Predsokratovci Platón, zv.1), p. 118).

Peter Sýkora suggests several possible translations (interpretations) of Parmenides' statement: *"What exists is at the same time conceivable."*

Or perhaps:
"What is not conceivable does not exist."
"If it is conceivable, it also exists."
Maybe, the relation of mind and existence, as seen by Parmenides, can be summarized as follows:

What is not thinkable in terms of ideas (logic) is not thinkable (cannot exist) ontologically (Sýkora, Ontológia šera, p. 61).

It is not surprising that Parmenides did not have, except for Plotinus, a follower and improver of his conception. Plato did not question the main ideas of his arguments: the variety of the world perceived by us is only an illusion but then Plato digresses from Parmenides: plurality of the world of ideas really exists. Aristotle in his treatise, Metaphysics, coped with Parmenides' statement that being and The One are the same and he refuted it. He did not doubt the existence of objective reality. It was only in the 17th century that an author appeared who accepted Parmenides' statements and developed them. It was Spinoza, the author of Ethics. In this treatise, Spinoza postulates the substance (Parmenidian "eon") which is unchangeable, immovable, indivisible, and uncreated. Movement, plurality and the like are only its manifestations.

Subjects to think about:

Try dealing with Parmenides' main thesis on the non-existence of plurality of beings. What counter-arguments against his statements can you think of? How can you cope with coming to deadlock: there is no plurality of beings but without it we are not able to know anything, to say anything…

Recommended literature:

Solomon, R.: The Big Questions. A Short Introduction to Philosophy, pp. 117-120.
The Routledge Companion to Metaphysics, pp. 10-12

5. Time and Events in the Greeks. Pre-Socratic Philosophers and Plato

The basics of Greek cosmology can already be found in Homer's works. Schadewaldt analyses the 18th book of the Iliad where Hephaestus forges armour for Achilles as a base for Greek ontology and cosmology. The picture of the world is here in the shape of a circle. There is Earth's plate in the middle, around Oceanus, and the canopy of the heavens in the shape of a hemisphere above it (see: Schadewaldt, Von Homers Welt und Werk. Aufsatze und Auslegungen Zur Homerischen Frage, 1944). Homer's picture of the world represents a threefold division: heaven, Earth, and the underworld which correspond to the division of the gods according to the parts of the world which they rule. Zeus controls the heavens, Hades the underworld, and Poseidon the sea. The Earth is common to everyone (see: Schadewaldt, 1944). *"Thinking about the world in the oldest time strives for a clear order.*

We observe that...existence of being appears in such basic categories which are delimited both mythically and ontologically" (Schadewaldt, 1944).

The myth of cosmic cycles gained control over the thinking of pre-Socratic philosophers too. It is obvious, for example, in Anaximander according to whom, everything was born from apeiron and everything will return to it. Empedocles imagined the events in the cosmos as an alternating prevalence of two principles – filia and neikos; creation and destruction of the cosmos which continues without end. Plato perceives the passage of cosmic time from a similar perspective. He dealt with this topic in a dialog called The Statesman. The cause of cosmic return is, according to him, a double movement of the universe. *"There was a time when God directed the revolutions of the world, but at the end of a certain cycle he let go; and the world, by the necessity of its nature, turned back, and went around the other way. For divine things alone are unchangeable; but the earth and heavens, although endowed with many glories, have a body, and are therefore liable to perturbation. In the case of the world, the perturbation is very slight, and amounts only to a reversal of motio"* (Plato: Politicus, 269 d). The universe, according to Plato, still *"...remains ever unchanged and the same, and body is not included in this class. Heaven and the universe, as we have termed them, although they have been endowed by the Creator with many glories, partake of a bodily nature, and therefore cannot be entirely free from perturbation. But their motion is, as far as possible, single and in the same place, and of the same kind; and is therefore only subject to a reversal, which is the least alteration possible"* (Plato: Politicus, s. 269 e, p. 431).

But the rotation itself, according to Plato, is proper only for God but even he does not have the right to move the universe once this way and once that way. The change of direction is accompanied by a great cataclysm, a great extinction of animals occurs and even mankind is reduced along with many strange conditions appearing: *"For their life was reversed like the motion of the world, and first of all coming to a stand then quickly returned to youth and beauty. The white locks of the aged became black; the cheeks of the bearded man were restored to their youth and fineness"* (Plato: Politicus, 270 e, 432). Old men coming back to the condition of children in mind can be, in Plato's opinion, the result of the dead, who are lying in the ground, coming back to life, and following the reversal of development. At this time, a generation of the "sons of the Earth" (gegeneis) was born (see: Eliade, p. 102). There were neither beasts nor hatred among animals, men did not have women or children, they did not unite in communities or families, all of them rose from the earth to life.

The myth of the primary paradise, which was implied by Plato, is present also in Indian thinking, and in Iranian and Jewish tradition (messianic *illud tempus*). This concept, more or less, copies the archaic idea of paradise inception. Besides the traditional mythological ideas, Babylonian influences can be found in the dialog, The Statesman: *"Plato imputes periodic cataclysms to planetary revolutions, an explanation that certain recent research would derive from Babylonian astronomical speculation"* (Eliade, p. 103).

Stoicism inspired, on one hand, by Heraclitus and, on the other hand, by eastern gnosis, also worked with the idea of the "great year" and cosmic fire *ekpyrósis* which regularly destroys the cosmos and subsequently restores it again. The motif of eternal return controls the entire Graeco-Roman culture. According to Matúš Porubjak, the thoughts of an archaic man are close to memory (see Porubjak, p. 54). *"Decision making – thinking – contemplating an archaic hero is basically recalling memories"* (Porubjak, p. 54). This contemplation reminds us rather of reflecting, it is not thinking "forward" but an effort to remember the original archetypes and how predecessors dealt with any given satiation. The periodic restoration of the cosmos, *metakosmésis,* was popular with the new Pythagorean philosophers.

The myth about *apokatastasis,* a return to the beginning was, on the other hand, popular in Hellenism after Alexander the Great. Whether it is a case of metakosmésis or apokatastasis, both ideas are connected by an antihistorical approach. The above mentioned myth about cosmic fire had its biggest success in the Graeco-Eastern environment. Its origin can probably be traced to Iran.

This myth (from which Jewish-Christian culture derives its eschatology and apocalypses of stoicism) was, strange as it sounds, comforting. Because the fire restores the world, rids it of old age, death, destruction. As stated by Eliade it is a case of apokarastasis of which the just do not have to be afraid (see: Eliade, p. 105). For example, an Iranian concept says that history is not eternal, it does not repeat, one day it will come an end in a cataclysmic *ekpyrósis.* This final disaster represents, on one hand, the end of history and, on the other, its settlement. *"It is then in illo tempore that, as we are told, all will render an account of what they have done „in history" and only those who are not guilty will know beatitude and eternity"* (Eliade, p. 106).

These Iranian ideas greatly influenced the Christian apologist Lactantius (full name Lucius Caecilius Firmianus Lactantius). God created the world in six days and the seventh day he rested so the universe will last six millennia during which the Earth will be ruled by evil. In the seventh millennium the demon will be fettered and mankind will live in peace for the next thousand years. Then the demon will free himself from the chains and he will lead a war against the just who will overpower him in the end. In the eighth millennium, the world will be created anew, forever (see: Eliade, p. 106). Prophecies predicting the end of the world (the first one will be the fall of Rome) appear mainly in the Jewish-Christian Apocalypse but it was also known in Iran.

Lactantius predicted, similar to the Iranians (e.g. Persian apocalyptic text Bahman – Yašt) that a year will shorten, a month will be reduced, and day will be narrowed.

This is a vision of a cosmic lapse which is similar to a vision of a human lapse from India where in the prophecies the human age will be shortened from 80000 to 100 years. This period will be a time when mountains will slip down, people will long for death, and each tenth person will survive: *"...justice will be rejected and innocence disdained, the evil will lunge at the good with hostility, nobody will honour patches of grey, neither women nor children, all things will be mixed against god's and natural law"* (Lactanius, p. 278).

After the disasters, a clear fire will descend and establish blessedness, a golden age, the birth of a new world.

We can simply say that history is, just as for the Iranian so for the Jewish-Christian tradition, limited and the end of the world is identical with resurrection and victory of eternity over impermanence. And no matter how the position of a human was different in the individual concepts, they always had a common characteristic. Man could bear them because they were meaningful and, in the core, necessary. Historical drama was inevitable both for those who believed in cyclical repetition and for those who were convinced that there was only one cycle, which was coming to an end.

Reflections to think about:

Try to think over a concept (approach to) of historical events which are completely different from the pre-Socratic one. Can you find a concept in the history of philosophy which, on the contrary, results from the pre-Socratic one?

Recommended literature:

Aristotle: The Organon. 2011, Nabu Press.
Carr, B.: Metaphysics: An Introduction. Humanities Press International, 1987.
Kant, I.: The Critique of Pure Reason. Digireads.com Publishing, 2004.

6. Metaphysics as a Categorical Description

The subject of metaphysics is, according to some philosophical conceptions (e.g. Aristotle, Kant, Hegel, and Hartmann), the most basic aspects of our reality declaration about how we see the world. We usually divide the world into a complex structure of various kinds of things. We speak of plants, animals, people, means of transport, cities, etc. The basic divisions, which result from our perception of reality, are the subject of conceptions which analyse metaphysics as a categorical description (Carr, 1987).

Let us compare how two paradigmatic authors, Aristotle and Kant, deal with the categories.

6.1. Aristotelian Categories

Aristotle in the treatise Categories (Statements), which he wrote before Metaphysics, states ten categories: *"Expressions which are in no way composite signify substance, quantity, quality, relation, place, time, position, state, action, or affection. To sketch my meaning roughly, examples of substance are ‚man' or ‚horse', of quantity, such terms as ‚two cubits long' or ‚three cubits long', of quality, such attributes as ‚white', ‚grammatical'. ‚Double', ‚half', ‚greater', fall under the category of relation; ‚in the market place', ‚in the Lyceum', under that of place; ‚yesterday', ‚last year', under that of time. ‚Lying', ‚sitting', are terms indicating position, ‚shod', ‚armed', state; ‚to lance', ‚to cauterize', actions; ‚to be lanced', ‚to be cauterized', affections"* (Aristotle, The Categories, 2009).

All the things, beings which exist, can be, according to Aristotle, divided into the ten above mentioned categories. The first category, substance or ousia (from Greek) has a privileged position; it is unique because it exists independently, a bearer of qualities. The Greek ousia originally meant ownership, immovable property such as land, buildings, and others.

Aristotle defines the first and the second substance in the fifth book of categories in the following way.

"Substance, in the truest and primary and most definite sense of the word, is that which is neither predicable of a subject nor present in a subject; for instance, the indi-

vidual man or horse. But in a secondary sense those things are called substances within which, as species, the primary substances are included; also those which, as genera, include the species. For instance, the individual man is included in the species 'man', and the genus to which the species belongs is 'animal'; these, therefore—that is to say, the species 'man' and the genus 'animal,-are termed secondary substances" (Aristotle, The Categories, 2009).

The first substance is thus the particular "some this," Greek "tode ti," a particular book, a particular John Doe. The second substances are qualities which do not exist independently but always only as qualities of a substance. How did Aristotle come to his ten categories? By examining how we speak about beings around us, how we divide reality around us. As a result, Aristotle is called a *realist* or a *categorical realist* since his categories, which describe being, delimit real species which can be found in reality. Aristotelian categories are a matter of the world, they reflect reality.

6.2. Kant's Categories

Aristotelian categories were not accepted by all writers (although they were accepted for a long time). Immanuel Kant tackled them critically. His influential shift in understanding of categories as something that is not a matter of reality but a matter of us, who recognise this reality, resulted in the diminution of borders between ontology and epistemology. In his opinion, there are twelve categories or "pure concepts of understanding" which he divided into four groups: the quantity category (unity, plurality, totality), the quality category (reality, negation, limitation); the relation categories (substance and accident, cause and effect, reciprocity), and the modality categories (possibility, existence, necessity) (Kant, The Critique of Pure Reason, 2004).

Kant's categories are related to the creation of terms. The creation of terms means connecting of contents, or more precisely, signs, judging. A classification of forms of judging includes, in Kant, four levels where each of them consists of three forms of judgements. Kant finds in these forms basic forms of thinking. He did not come to these categories by means of the examination of reality, which is independent from our thoughts. Reality as such is out of our reach and the categories are therefore derived from another source: from logic (Carr, Metaphysics: An Introduction (Modern Introduction to Philosophy), 1987).

Forms of judgements which Kant adopted with some modification from traditional logic:

1. quantity: universal, particular, singular
2. quality: affirmative, negative, infinite
3. relation: categorical, hypothetical, disjunctive
4. modality: problematic, assertoric, apodictic

Let us give some examples for a better understanding:

A universal judgement: All people are mortal.
A particular judgement: Some people are philosophers.
A singular judgement: Kant was a philosopher.
An affirmative judgement: Kant was an exceptional philosopher.
A negative judgement: Kant was not a molecular biologist.
An infinite judgement: Kant was a non-realist. (This type of judgement remains open for many possibilities, this judgement does not state what Kant was in a positive sense).
A categorical (unconditioned) judgement: This triangle has a right angle.
A hypothetical (conditioned) judgement: If a triangle has one right angle, are the other two sharp.
A disjunctive (excluding) judgement: A triangle is either right-angled, acute, or obtuse.
A problematic judgement: Maybe it is going to rain today.
An assertoric (confirming) judgement: It will rain today.

An apodictic (necessary) judgement: It has to rain today (Kant's analysis of the forms of judgements can be, with examples, found in the works of W.O. Döring: *Das Lebenswerk Immanuel Kants*, 1947, Hamburg, pp. 47-48).

In order to define his categories Kant did change his mindset towards reality, as Carr says: *"...it is a case of fundamental forms of thinking which are the embodied forms of judgements. This fact contrasts Kant with Aristotle, for whom categories were, no matter how they were identified, natural,, real divisions of things in the world"* (Carr, 1987).

6.3. More Recent Reflections

In the twentieth century a conviction appeared, together with the emergence of the philosophy of language, that our thinking is connected with language. It follows that language is the tool which makes an unseizable "reality as such" into an understandable and seizable "reality for us." An Aristotelian examination of the world and Kant's thinking about the structure of our thoughts loses a good justification. What should be done? A grammatical analysis of language. As suggested by Jaroslav Peregrin, language analysis does not concern only the categories as the highest level of our conceptual apparatus but lower levels as well: *"...if we want, for example, to find out whether it makes any sense to talk about the existence of something like numbers, there is no other possibility than to examine the function of these things within our language"* (Peregrin, p. 35).

An American analytical philosopher, W.V.O. Quine, went even further, according to him, we should completely reject questions such as "do the things of this and that category exist?" because they are meaningful only in the context of a certain language. He relativised ontology this way and lost its good justification. Ontology and grammar are in his opinion: *"...a part of our own conceptual contribution to our theory of the world"* (Quine, p. 44).

Reflections to think about:

Try to compare Aristotelian and Kantian categories, the approaches of both authors to the formation of categories and use arguments for a concept which corresponds with your conviction about reality and its understanding, or more precisely, its categorisation. Do you find any shortcomings in the suggested projects?

Recommended literature:

Aristotle: The Organon. 2011, Nabu Press.
Carr, B.: Metaphysics: An Introduction. Humanities Press International, 1987.
Kant, I.: The Critique of Pure Reason. Digireads.com Publishing, 2004.

7. Criticism of Metaphysics

Relativization or even criticism of metaphysics emerges from the previous chapter. Of course, the criticism of metaphysics already existed before the twentieth century. It was suggested in Kant's "Copernican revolution" in the previous chapter, but we can go farther back in the history of philosophy. For example, in the time of the Renaissance a strong anti-metaphysical approach emerged in several authors: Pico della Mirandola, Erasmus of Rotterdam, Michel de Montaigne, Francesco Petrarca, and others. Their criticism concerned a particular type of metaphysics, in particular scholastic metaphysics. The mentioned authors perceive metaphysics as a disadvantageous discipline because it does not allow any specific knowledge, it even completely lacks humility when determining the borders of human knowledge. A legitimate approach suggested by the Renaissance critics was scepticism. Erasmus of Rotterdam brilliantly expressed the vanity of metaphysics in his treatise *In Praise of Folly*: *"And these most subtle subtleties are rendered yet more subtle by the several methods of so many Schoolmen, that one might sooner wind himself out of a labyrinth than the entanglements of the realists, nominalists, Thomists, Albertists, Occamists, Scotists. Nor have I named all the several sects, but only some of the chief; in all which there is so much doctrine and so much difficulty that I may well conceive the apostles, had they been to deal with these new kind of divines, had needed to have prayed in aid of some other spiri."* (The Praise of Folly, p. 87).

Later, with the commencement of more sophisticated natural scientific research and inductive method the criticism of traditional metaphysics becomes stronger. According to authors like Isaac Newton, Voltaire, Schiller, Goethe, Francis Bacon, Rousseau, Diderot, and others metaphysics slows down the progress of knowledge. But not only that, criticism of this period penetrated into the social-political sphere. Metaphysics interconnected with religious (or more precisely ecclesiastical) power stood in the way of the ideals of the French Revolution and of the creation of a liberal state (Schmidinger, 2010).

Moreover, English empiricists and subsequently the already mentioned Kant coped critically with metaphysics. The development of metaphysics was harmful for cultural and educational progress, metaphysics lacked a gnoseological base (our knowledge is not able to capture reality as a whole) and is thus meaningless. It is not a science in the true sense of the word, as was argued by Hume (see Hume, D.: An Enquiry Concerning Human Understanding).

Another type of anti-metaphysical approach was later held by Friedrich Nietzsche. As far as the metaphysical approach is concerned, he did not like the fact that it makes it impossible for a human to live spontaneously: *"...so I speak to those from the otherworld... It was suffering and powerlessness – by means of them all other worlds were created"* (Nietzsche, Thus Spoke Zarathustra, 2005). Pragmatism was also critical to metaphysics. Wiliam James, who considered pragmatism to be mainly a method of solution of philosophical disputes, rejects abstraction, incorrect priory judgements, closed systems, and the supposed absolutes (see James W.: *Pragmatism*, 1975, Harvard University Press, 27-45).

Let us go back for a while to the philosophy of language and its approach by means of which metaphysics was relativised. Reality, the world can be, according to the followers of the philosophy of language, understood only if we understand the functions of language. The question or the problem is not based on "what is x" but on "what is the meaning of the word x?" or "how do we use the word x?" After the ontological turn to language, the question of the existence of an extra lingual reality was lost in the analysis of language as was pointed out by Peter Sýkora (Sýkora, p.35). Due to Kant's problematisation of metaphysics, the current metaphysics came to the question "Does it have to be applicable to everybody that which is applicable to me?" It results from this question and similar ones that we have to be content with resignation when looking for a consensus, or more precisely, for commensurability. However, we can end up in absolute utmost relativism where "everybody has his own truth."

7.1. Metaphysics and Postmodernism

With the commencement of postmodernism came a strong rejection of the optimism of Enlightenment, faith in progress, in the power of human knowledge and spirit, the questioning of "objectivity" which was in the Enlightenment very accepted emerges. Moreover, postmodern ontology is characterised by: difference, fragmentation, reality, plurality of methods, even radical plurality (see e.g. Welsch, W.: Unsere postmoderne Moderne, 2008, Walter de Gruyter, p.9, pp. 65-87).

Reflections to think about:

Do you sympathise with postmodern relativisation in metaphysics and ontology, with its relativising approach to "objective reality?" With which of the mentioned critical approaches do you have the most sympathy and why? Try to find in literature other anti-metaphysical conceptions which were not mentioned in this chapter.

Recommended literature:

James, W.: Pragmatism, 1975, Harvard University Press.
Welsch, W.: Unsere postmoderne Moderne, 2008, Walter de Gruyter.

8. Metaphysics as a Way to God

8.1. Negative Theology of Dionysius the Areopagite

The historians of medieval philosophy can argue about the authenticity of the medieval faith; however, they agree on one fact: if there is a concept which concentrates in itself all of the ideas of medieval people about the universe then this concept must be God. According to Le Goff, "we cannot find a more global and universal idea as this one. God embraces, or more correctly, floods the entire conceivable area of experience, everything that can be observed in nature or among people, everything that can be thought of, begins with the idea of God itself" (Le Goff, Time, Work, and Culture in the Middle Ages, 1980).

Dionysius the Areopagite made his mark in history, on one hand, with his teachings about the hierarchical order of the world (probably even the term *hierarchia* comes from him), with his teaching about sacraments, beauty, the interpretation of Biblical symbols but mainly with the method of negative (απογατικη) and positive (καταγατικη) theology.

A key topic of most of his works is the relationship between God and humans, a specific question of how (if at all) a human can know God. God is, in his understanding, separated from everything, a transcendent principle of everything that is (see: Koudelka, M.: Nauka o pozitivní a negativní theologii v Dionysiových Listech a Mystické theologii. In: Dionysios Areopagity: Listy. O mystické theologii. Praha: OIKOYMENH, 2005, p. 11). This definition says that God is elevated above everything (negative approach) and at the same time it says that God is the cause of the entire reality (positive approach).

In *Letters* and *Divine Names*, Dionysius trifles with a metaphor of dark and light, ignorance and knowledge, and he uses Plato's parable about the sun and explains in which way God can be marked as *the good*. For Dionysius, the name "good" is the most dignified designation of God because it can best relate to his essence. *"Because of his benignity, God is not closed in his otherness but he causes everything to exist"* (Koudelka, p. 26).

Likewise, the Sun is perceived as a clear picture and symbol of God's benignity since it is the source of existence of the earthly world and it allows us to see. The effect of the good (light) is reflected in Dionysius's teachings about evil. Evil is understood, in accordance with the early medieval tradition, as a decrease, the absence of good, in Dionysius's terminology defined as *absence of light, darkness.* The good, light, is according to Dionysius, linked with darkness. It means that at the sensual level darkness represents the absence of light (physical), at the spiritual level the absence of light is a symbol of *sin, fall, ignorance.* Light is in our common life seen as something extremely positive, superior to darkness. Dionysius regards it as being superior to darkness which does not have its own cause – darkness cannot arise from the Sun, evil cannot come from good. Darkness is (so far) for him an absolute negativity. The introductory sentences of the first Letter addressed to the monk Gaius: *"Darkness becomes invisible by light, and especially by much light. Varied knowledge, and especially much varied knowledge, makes the Agnosia vanish"* (Dionysios Areopagita, 2005).

In the next lines of *Letters* a sudden, even surprising, change in the interpretation of darkness emerges. Darkness stops being understood in a traditional sense as a decrease, a lack of the good or light and begins to be something that extends beyond light.

Non-knowledge begins, this way, to be a deeper kind of thinking which brings more penetrating results. Starting with the third sentence of the first Letter by Dionysius, the reader is confronted with an insufficient way of light which accompanies the positive way to God and with fierce criticism of everybody who clings to beings (See mainly Letters I-VI: Dionysios Areopagita, 2005).

A note on the term "being." Dionysius does not mean with this term the material beings but the area of intelligent existence, since intelligent existence is for him the primary and actually existing one, the rest is subject to change and end so it seems to be a "nonbeing." Dionysius addressed the analysis of what is and what is not in the treatise; Mystical Theology to Timotheus (See: *O mystickej theologii Timotheovi* I 1). At first sight, it can be problematic for our minds: the terms light, good, brightness, intellect, and existence are common names for God. Dionysius does not deny that these names are more appropriate than those which exist in the material sphere but they are inadequate in the same way. They cannot understand God for the same reason as material things – God is after all outside existence, he is above existence.

We, as God's creations, can know God in a certain way but we should be aware of the fact that we can know him only as far as he lets us. As has been mentioned above, according to Dionysius, God cannot be named *the good* (although this name is the most apt one), because he is more than the good, more than the light, he is unapproachable light, darkness. "The Divine gloom is the unapproachable light in which God is said to dwell. And in this gloom, invisible indeed, on account of the surpassing brightness, and unapproachable on account of the excess of the super-essential stream of light" (Dionysios Areopagita, 2005).

It is possible to move closer to the God who transcends every being, existence, and knowledge only by means of *non-knowledge*. The way of non-knowledge is grounded in the understanding of the fact that God is nothing of what is. It does not mean an absolute rejection of the positive way. *"Negative theology is not incompatible with positive theology"* (Koudelka, p. 29).

Affirmative and negative way can seem to be as opposite; however, for Dionysius they are only different approaches which can be used by a human to get closer to God (and to himself). It is characteristic for affirmative (cataphatic) theology that God shows himself to us by means of his manifestations in the world of beings. The positive, affirmative, or cataphatic theology has its legitimacy in the praise of God as a creator and in the interpretation of God's names in the Holy Scripture. To express a positive approach, the positive statements, *thesis*, are used. God can be ascribed with the names of all things by means of the names of the thesis. He can be then named stone, cloud, warm, cold, small, tall, and the like, so it means even the most surprising or the least noble. The affirmative approach says a lot about the multi-nameness (polynomos). Declarations about God would, according to Dionysius, still be insufficient no matter how extensive the list of positive thesis. Dionysius's descending way in affirmative theology starts with the noblest names and "more appropriate ones" and ends with the most inappropriate names. *"And, it is necessary, as I think, to celebrate the abstractions in an opposite way to the definitions. or, we used to place these latter by beginning from the foremost and descending through the middle to the lowest"* (Dionysios Areopagita, 2005). The noblest names are, in accordance with the then patristic tradition, the names which are connected with the immanent Divine province which means The One, The Trinity, The Father, The Son, and The Ghost. The moderately appropriate are intelligible names like the good, existence, truth, love, and the like. And at last, the most undignified designations of God are those which can be derived from the individual material things perceptible through senses – a stone, cloud, and the like. Positive theology represents the descent (katabasis), decreasing way, manifestation of God from his most perfect demonstrations. This way is characterised by God's influence in the variety of the realm of senses.

Dionysius understands the entire reality in a hierarchical way (allegedly the term hierarchy originates from him) and an attentive reader could notice a certain hierarchy in the affirmations themselves. In the case of positive *thesis,* it is necessary to start with the most dignified ones – designations which are closest to God. Positive theology is based on the constantly expanding number of *thesis* while negative theology has to be brief and based on the minimum number of negative designations. In the positive approach, the entire decline ends with the wealth of language since its primary goal is to praise the greatness of God, the creator of the intelligible and sensual world.

With his apophatic approach Dionysius is not trying to depict what God is but rather he is trying to point out what God is not. This method is performed by means of replacing (ajaireiV) all the determinations which were assigned to God by the affirmative approach. He goes even further, as far as to deny the of being of God to anyone who is neither from the sensual world nor anything intellectual or intelligible. Dionysius applies the ablating to all names used by the positive approach, even to the noblest ones.

Dionysius put, in the negative approach, stress on God's transcendentality; God is above everything in a way that exceeds all existence. He is absolutely different, unknowable, and unnameable. While the entire way of the positive approach was completed with the plurality of names of God, God is, according to Dionysius, nameless (anomos) the negative theology. How would it be possible to speak about God in this way?

"We say then- that the Cause of all, which is above all, neither without being, nor without life—nor with- out reason, nor without mind, nor is a body—nor has shape—nor form—nor quality, or quantity, or bulk—nor is it in a place—nor is seen—nor has sensible contact—nor per-

ceives, nor is perceived, by the senses—nor has disorder and confusion, as being vexed by earthly passions,—nor is powerless, as being subject to casualties of sense,—nor is in need of light;—neither is It, nor has It, change, or decay, or division, or deprivation, or flux,—or any other of the objects of sense" (Dionysios Areopagita, 2005).

The completion of negative theology lies in exceeding the limits of language (also the metaphorical one), in the absence of words, in silence, and quiet.

Above-intellective knowledge can be reached if we do not get to know anything and then just using non-knowledge we praise God. It would be erroneous to think that the negative approach, in which we take everything away, ends with emptiness. *"If it relates to God as non-existence, it does not mean the degradation and emptying of the divinity or its non-existence"*(Koudelka, p. 30). Here it is necessary to draw the reader's attention to various specifications of Dionysius's manipulation with the term darkness.

In the first *Letter*, when he writes about darkness in connection with God, it cannot be understood as privation as it was understood at the intellective level (see: List I). God is *without being,* his existence goes beyond being, it is as though *a surplus of being.* The right knowledge of God, which is at the end of the road of negative theology, shows a God who is neither knowable nor recognisable but he is *more* than knowable. He is neither polyonymous nor nameless but he is above all names.

The central motif of the negative way to God is henósis (ενωσις), a unification of human and God. First, the human needs to know that the existing light hides darkness which the human seeks to know. This darkness is, according to Dionysius, the real true light. The one who follows the way of negative theology has to cross beyond the sphere of the sensorially perceptible and the intelligible, has to free himself from everything needless, reject even existence as such because its light covers the nonexistence (above-existence) of God.

In order to know what exceeds the intellect, Dionysius advises us to stop our intellectual activities. Such above-intellectual knowledge is not common human knowledge. It is rather an adequate non-knowledge of what, or more precisely, of whom we get to know; non-knowledge adequate for God. Dionysius considers it to be knowledge of a higher kind. Due to it, the superluminous substance in which God is hidden is uncovered.

The unification of human and God is possible at the higher level than the sphere of human abilities. It is therefore an erroneous conclusion that we can know God. Those living with this presumption cannot ever get to know God. A human must simply understand that *"effort to understand in a human way what lies beyond its borders is necessarily in vain"* (Dionysios Areopagita, 2005). It can seem at first sight that if we are not able to approach God with reason, he remains absolutely unapproachable for us. Dionysius' method henósis disproves these misapprehensions while unification is *superordinate* to knowing. If we want to get to know God it is not sufficient to let go of only the sensual and knowable things, we have to give up all our most individual abilities and ourselves too. *"It is he most Divine knowledge of the Almighty God, within the union beyond mind, when the mind, having stood apart from all existing things, and then, having dismissed itself, has been united to the superluminous rays—thence and there, being illuminated by the unsearchable wisdom"* (Dionysios Areopagita, 2005).

The last of Dionysius' authored works dedicated to negative theology is represented by a short treatise *Mystic Theology*. Despite quite a small scope this work became a co-creating treatise of European philosophy and theology and Dionysius was elevated to the position of a respected author due to this work. This treatise also includes symbols of darkness – non-knowledge and light – knowledge. In *Mystical Theology*, Dionysius emphasises that for him negative theology does not only represent means to assist him in order to get to his goal – unification with God. The affirmative and negative theology serve to celebrate God, they are *hymnology*. While he is describing an appropriate way of praising God by means of negative theology he uses a metaphor adopted from Plotinus: *"Those who make a lifelike statue, by extracting all the encumbrances which have been placed upon the clear view of the concealed, and by bringing to light, by the mere cutting away, the genuine beauty concealed in it"* (Dionysios Areopagita, 2005).

If Dionysius wants to know God in the most adequate way, he has to get rid of all his covers and veils which could disturb the contact with God. A sculptor hewing a stone with his tools and uncovering hidden beauty can be considered a metaphor which clearly describes the ascending negative theology.

8.2. Theocentrism of J. S. Eriugena

Negative theology very strongly influenced an author who translated Dionysius's works into Latin: Johannes Scotus Eriugena. He was active in the ninth century and in a treatise Periphyseon or *The Division of Nature* (De divisione naturae) he divides being, "nature," into four development phases:

- Nature which is not created and does not create (anarchos): God without beginning
- Nature which creates and is not created: archetypal world of primary
- Nature which is created and does not create: the arrangement of animate and inanimate nature
- Nature which is not created and no longer creates (reditus): God as a goal of everything

"Nature" which Eriugena writes about does not mean only physics but mainly the naturalness of all things, as it was pointed out by de Libera (See: de Libera, A.: Středověká filosofie, pp. 272-277).

The treatise is divided into five books. In the first book, Eriugena dealt with the application of the ten categories of God and in the others he interprets the book of Genesis. His conception is theocentric. Divine existence stands in the centre and develops everything according to itself.

8.3. Ontological Proof of God according to Anselm of Canterbury

The fact that the "proof," or more precisely, searching for various approaches which could prove the existence of God was very fashionable in the Middle Ages is demonstrated by a popular "ontological proof" of Anselm of Canterbury who lived in the eleventh century. His effort is characteristic of a manifesto "faith seeking understanding," *fides quaerens intellectum* (de Libera, p. 292).

In the treatise *Proslogion*, he presented an argument which should disprove the declaration of a biblical madman who in the 13th psalm claims that "there is no God." He works on the assumption that God is something above the highest thing it is possible to think of, that God is the maximum of maximums. Such definition of God could be accepted even by atheists, which means that God exists at least in our minds. He considers further that there is a concept in our mind which exceeds us, the imperfect beings. God as a concept which describes the infinite perfection in our finite mind.

On the basis of the above mentioned he concludes that:

It is not possible to imagine God's nonexistence because what necessarily exists is more perfect than what can be imagined as non-existent and thus it exists only accidentally. The idea of perfection is connected with real existence. The thing above the highest thing it is possible to think of has to necessarily exist (see Anselm, Wiliams, T.: *Proslogion: With the Replies of Gaunilo and Anselm,* 2001, Hacket Publishing, p. 1-27).

Or in another way:
It is necessary to find a central part between two statements
- 1. I understand what God would be if he existed
- 2. God exists

Anselm's goal is not the existence or idea, as de Liberta points out, but maximum.

"Hence, if that-than-which-a-greater-cannot-be-thought can be thought to not exist, then that-than-which-a-greater-cannot-be-thought is not the same as that-than-which-a-greater-cannot-be-thou, which is absurd. Something-than-which-a-greater-cannot-be-thought exists so truly then,

that it cannot be even though not to exist. And You, Lord our God, are this being" (Proslogion, in: Sokol J.: Mistr Eckhart a středověká mystika, Praha, 1993, pp.77-100). Let us add that Anselm's proof of existence of God was considered to be an *ontological* argument by Kant (at the time of Anselm's activity the term ontology was unknown and there was no difference between existence and essence).

8.4. Five Ways to God of Thomas Aquinas

Probably the most important scholastic thinker, St. Thomas Aquinas included in his works rational arguments by means of which we are able to get to the existence of God. They resemble the Aristotelian characteristics of the unmoved mover. Aquinas finds these five ways (quinque viae) to God:

2. God is the cause of movement: everything that moves has to start and end its movement in something that does not move itself
3. God is the cause of causes: a similar argument as the previous one, God does not have any cause outside himself and causes as a cause of other things.
4. God is necessity: God cannot not be, the other, accidental beings receive existence from him.
5. God is at the top of the hierarchy: creatures are hierarchically ordered and God is at the top.

6. God is the final purpose of everything: this idea reminds us of Eriugena's understanding of God as redit; creatures realise their possibilities and completion is included in God.

(see: Owens, J.: *Saint Thomas Aquinas on the Existence of God: The Collected Papers of Joseph Owens*, 1980, Sunny Press).

Reflections to think about:

Try to find counter-arguments against all the mentioned "proofs," approaches, and ways in which to prove the existence of God in this chapter. With which "proof" do you agree the most and why?

Recommended literature:

Anselm, Wiliams, T.: Proslogion: With the Replies of Gaunilo and Anselm, 2001, Hacket Publishing, pp. 1-27.
Pseudo-Dionysios: The complete Works. 1987. Paulist Press.

9. Problems of the Universals

An argument about universals can undoubtedly be considered the most important landmark in the entire history of western culture (Schmidinger, 2010).

It followed an entirely new relationship of humans to reality. At first, the argument was of an metaphysical-gnoseological character: can it be found in the reality *universale*, which means generally? The universals, e.g. "rose as such," "dog as such," and the like. A problem was if: *"...anything corresponds to the thing which we assign the conceptual (conceptus), or more precisely, general (universale), which means whether is there anything in the reality itself, anything real and existing, an opposite to the conceptual one and general one in our approach"* (Schmidinger, 2010).

While dealing with this argument, two main attitudes were crystallised:

1. Realism (Platonists, Aristotelians, Thomists) which says that universals really exist, or better to say, something in the being itself corresponds to them. They identified the general with essence, or rather, with form (see e.g.: http://plato.stanford.edu/entries/universals-medieval/).

"Words are signs of ideas, and ideas the similitude of things, it is evident that words relate to the meaning of things signified through the medium of the intellectual conception.... Thus the name „man" expresses the essence of man in himself, since it signifies the definition of man by manifesting his essence.... And because in creatures of this kind what is perfect and subsistent is compound; whereas their form is not a complete subsisting thing, but rather is that whereby a thing is; hence it follows that all names used by us to signify a complete subsisting thing must have a concrete meaning as applicable to compound things; whereas names given to signify simple forms, signify a thing not as subsisting, but as that whereby a thing is; as, for instance, whiteness signifies that whereby a thing is white" (Aquinas, Summa Theologica, p. 107-108).

2. Nominalism (William Ockham, Gilbert of Poitiers, Roscelinus of Compiègne) which claims that the universals do not exist, they are only concepts which help our mind abstract. Reason creates either general thoughts (conceptus); a branch of nominalism – a so-called conceptualism originates from there; or names (nomen), sounds (flatus vocis), from there a so-called vocalism.

The argument between nominalism and realism was especially serious and, particularly in the thirteenth and fourteenth century, a highly escalated dispute. Because if we accept the opinion of the nominalists that everything general exists only in the form of language, or more precisely, sound, it is only a question of time before it is applied to the subject of metaphysics, which means reality, God, existence and the like. This approach is highly suspicious and unacceptable for medieval philosophy.

For a better understanding, let us elaborate a little more on both conceptions using examples: for a realist there is something like essence, in the form of, let us say, a human. According to the nominalists there is only a concept of a human or a sound, when we say the word "human." There is always only one John Doe and not a general "human as such." Another example uses a triangle: according to realists, there is a universal triangle as such, the nominalists admit the existence of a particular triangle, e.g. the one on the blackboard, a particular equilateral or a particular right-angled or a particular triangle which is drawn in your exercise book.

The argument about universals is, for example, in biology *"...an argument about the existence of a biological species. The biological species is either a real existing entity (realism) or an aid for biologists and their orientation in the animated nature (nominalism)"* (Sýkora, p. 28).

Reflections to think about:

Try to state arguments for the foundation of both attitudes, both realism and nominalism. Then try the counter-argument. Which position is closer to yours and why? Try to find authors or conceptions in the literature which deal with this argument, or with its application, in current metaphysics and ontology.

Recommended literature:

http://plato.stanford.edu/entries/universals-medieval
Lagerlund, H.: Encyclopaedia of Medieval Philosophy: Philosophy Between 500 and 1500, Springer Science & Business Media, 2010.
Lagerlund, H.: Representation and Objects of Thought in Medieval Philosophy, Ashgate Publishing, 2012.

10. Metaphysics and Problem of Intuition. Henri Bergson

One of the key problems which stretch across the history of metaphysics and epistemology is the problem of intuition. More space will be devoted to it in this chapter by analysis of the approach of Henri Bergson.

Henri Bergson tried in his works to create a philosophical concept which would be based on *accuracy*. Philosophy, or traditional metaphysics, which he criticises, lacks accuracy. According to him, the traditional philosophical systems are not "tailored" to the reality in which we live. *"They are far too big for it"* (Bergson, H.: La pensée et le mouvant, 1969). These systems would fit into a world where there are not, besides people, any plants, animals and people do not need to sleep and eat, dream, the energy would not be consumed in this world but on the contrary, it would increase but the systems that are criticised by Bergson are so abstract that they can involve everything both possible and impossible.

Bergson based his metaphysics on a new approach to the evolution of life which took into account real time, or better to say, duration, passage, dynamics, and change. Bergson says that it is natural that science is not interested in duration since its function is to put the world together for us where we can cover the effects of time due to the simplicity of actions. Philosophy should approach duration in a different way. Bergson believes the whole problem of abstract philosophical systems lies in the fact that they placed time and space on an equal footing. They relied too much on intellect which is only able to capture a set of individual positions from duration; it reaches one point, then another and another.

He is looking for firmness, steadiness, it watches where the movable object is, which way it goes and where it will be. As long as metaphysics relies only on intellect, it remains a hypothetical construction. He chose a different way, diverged from associationism, Spencerian agnosticism, Comtian positivism, and at last he went so far that he denied even the Kantian conception of the relativity of knowledge (Bergson, 1969). Kant came to the conclusion that a "thing itself" is elusive, Bergson's analyses showed that there is at least one thing which can be understood in its entire naturalness, more specifically ourselves. "Our self becomes apparent in the way it is "itself" (en soi)..." (Bergson, 1969). At the beginning of the research we mentioned that Bergson focused mainly on accuracy and it is, according to him, not attainable by any other method than *intuition*. Bergson's philosophical concept is based on intuition and therefore his philosophy is known as *intuitivism.*

Bergson distinguished his method of intuition from that which was understood by other authors. "Bergsonian" intuition has very little in common with the irrational predictions with which it is often connected (Hrdlička, J.: *O intuici u Bergsona*. In: *Filosofie Henri Bergsona*. p.126). Bergson himself hesitated for a long time over whether to use the term intuition. "Intuition" is the word over which I hesitated for long time. From all the terms, that describe a certain way of thinking, it is the most apt; and yet it still causes a lack of clarity (Bergson, 1969). Bergson was aware of the difficulty of defining intuition so besides careful use of the term, he was critical too of language which, according to him, cannot capture intuition directly but can refer to it metaphorically: "Let nobody require a simple and geometric definition of intuition from me" (Bergson, 1969). The full definition of intuition cannot be pronounced directly in language.

Bergson gradually elevated intuition to method in his reflections. *"Intuition is the method of Bergsonism. Intuition is neither a feeling, an inspiration, nor a disorderly sympathy, but a fully developed method, one of the most fully developed methods in philosophy"* (Deleuze, G.: *Bergsonismus*, 2006, p.7).

How could intuition, which is predominantly a certain type of immediate knowing, create a method? After all, method fundamentally implies one or several mediations). (Deleuze, 2006) When answering this question, the explanation, that Bergson presents, intuition as a simple act, could help us (but this does not rule out qualitative multiplicity, the different directions in which it is executed).

10.1. Duration

Bergson's notion of intuition presupposes duration. As indicated above, reality can be understood only in motion; duration is the core of reality. If intuition jumped to the past, according to Bergson, it would mean that it would stay in the area of intellect and thus would replace intellectual terms with one which would cover them all. It would be a case of a hypothetical explanation of the entire reality. Bergson does not agree with this conception, on the contrary, he supports the intuitive metaphysics which would "...follow the wave motion of reality! It would not understand the totality of all things at once but on the contrary, each thing would be explained in such a way as it would exactly and exclusively adapt to reality. Reality would not start with a definition or a description of the unity of the systematic world: who knows whether there is really only one world?" (Bergson, 1969). Let us go back to the term duration since it is one of the key terms of Bergson's philosophy.

Duration in French is *durée*, the verb *durer* to last, persists the meaning of which is close to verbs, lie, do nothing, stay in a place. But Bergson has in mind the very opposite of this word – when he uses the expressions *durée, durer,* he speaks of constant change, evolution, life. *"A living being from the very core lasts; it lasts because it produces something without ceasing: this production cannot do without searching and searching without groping"* (Bergson, 1969). *To produce, search, grope* are not common synonyms for the verb *to last* (See: Markoš, A.: *Přírodní zákony a evoluce.* In: *Filosofie Henri Bergsona,* p.166). Bergson interprets the verb *durer* also to mean *to live.* Bergson's understanding of the expression *duration* is identical with (or close to) an expression *production, groping, living.* It is important to understand that, for Bergson, duration is indivisible, *"...time sequence cannot be understood as differentiation into "before" and "after;" that would mean to place them next to each other, which means, exchange for space"* (Kouba, P.: *Pohyb medzi časem a prostorem.* In: *Filosofie Henri Bergsona,* p. 92). The most famous example used by Bergson for pure duration is melody, which means, a sequence of tones which blend into one dynamic harmonic whole from which they cannot be separated into individual parts. In order to produce a melody we have to connect and divide the identical tones, we have to feel the difference between moments when one tone lasts and the tones which alternate at the same moment (Kouba, P.: *Pohyb medzi časem a prostorem*. In: *Filosofie Henri Bergsona*, p. 93). Neither *instinct* nor *intellect* are in a pure state. Bergson says that there is no intellect in which we could not find a trace of instinct and, in the same way, there is no instinct in which we could not find intellect.

Bergson rejects conceptions where instinct and intellect are considered to be qualities (mightiness) of one and the same order and the difference between them lies only in complicatedness. But in reality they complement each other (only by the mere fact that they are different methods of influence on a dead substance), even though they are different in the way of the realisation of their abilities. Intellect is a quality which *produces* and *changes* the produced. *"There are things that intelligence alone is able to seek, but which, by itself, it will never find. These things instinct alone could find; but it will never seek them"* (Bergson, L'évolution créatrice, 1966, p. 210). Intellect feels comfortable and free when it deals with dead substance. The most general quality of substance is vastness so intellect can then *"...without problems develop in space"* (Bergson, 1969).

When perceiving movement, the intellect occupies itself with the question of where a solid figure goes, it holds to its current or future positions but not to procedures by means of which the solid figure goes from one place to another; intellect does not deal with the movement itself, it comes out of the static and if it wants to imagine a movement it stops the solids at one of the static points which it put in order one next to the other, it is only able to make a *cinematographic model* of the world. Intellect is, according to Bergson, not adapted to think about development itself, which means continuity of change, since it imagines each event as a line of states which it divides into a new and more detailed sequence. It can disperse and reconstitute only by means of the given components which are *stable*. *"So that, though we may do our best to imitate the mobility of becoming by an addition that is ever going on, becoming itself slips through our fingers just when we think we are holding it tight"* (Bergson, L'évolution créatrice, 1966, p. 210). Intellect does not allow the unpredictable and creation.

As for the creation of the new, our intellect is able to understand it neither in its spurting (which means its indivisibility) nor in its brilliance (the creative). Intellect is made to use and control substance; its structure itself was, according to Bergson, shaped on the basis of a structure of substance. Bergson concludes that our intellect, however smart when dealing with the inanimate, handles the animated clumsily because it is inflexible, rigid, mechanical, and other deadening and violent methods. If intellect handles things mechanically, it acts organically.

Intellect uncovers, by means of its biggest works – science, more and more detailed physical processes but as for life (in other words duration), it can only provide us with a translation using concepts of the inanimate. Intellect moves around the examined subject.

Bergson compares intellect to a diver and instinct to a flyer in order to clarify the difference between intellect and instinct. The diver is at the bottom of the sea examining a shipwreck but the flyer drew his attention to it. In the same way an intellect immersed in concepts is analytically verifying point by point what constituted the subject of the synthetic perspective of intuition. Intellect firms and immobilises everything that it focuses its attention on. It looks away from the real duration.

According to Bergson, we do not *think about* duration but we *experience, live, and feel* it. It goes beyond intellect. *"It is not possible to reduce duration and life in Bergson's works into some frame because they are characterised by the continuation of frames, continuous increase and change. The frames are products of intellect but intuition is going against these frames"* (Hrdlička, J.: *O intuici u Bergsona*. In: *Filosofie Henri Bergsona*, p. 133). Bergson's intuition is in the duration, it is even possible to say that is the duration that was indicated at the beginning. To choose the intuitive method means to think about duration. If intuition jumped to eternity and freed itself from duration, it would stay in the area of intellect forever.

However, intellect and intuition are two different types of knowledge, it is necessary to bear in mind that Bergson does not see an impassable border between them; according to him, intellect and intuition complement each other in their activities. Intellect "sees" an impulse at which intuition pointed (similarly like in the example with a flyer and a diver), intellects acts like a blind man without intuition, there is a lot of material, products, and results around him, which he "does not see." We would not be able to systemise and put knowledge into practice only by means of intuition and without intellect. We would not be able to classify them.

But it is a mistake to think that we can go from one mightiness to another – according to Bergson, it is only possible to go from intuition to analysis but in no case the other way around. *"From the moments of changeability I can create as many variations, qualities or modifications as I like because they are all the motionless views of analysis on movability which is being ascribed to intuition. But if I put these modifications together it will never create anything that could resemble changeability because these modifications were not its parts but its components and that is something completely different"* (Bergson, L'évolution créatrice, 1966). Science and metaphysics come together in intuition (see Bergson, H.: *Matiére et mémoire,* p. 210). By creating a really intuitive philosophy we would come to the unity of these two different approaches, namely science and metaphysics. Metaphysics could even be made into a positive science, to the extent that, it would be able to make progress and it would help science to realise its own content. In the work Matter and Memory, Bergson defines metaphysics as a human spirit who: *"...is trying to free himself from the conditioned useful activities and get himself together as clear energy"* (Bergson, 1966). Bergson deeply and extensively analysed intellect and intuition with the aim to help us to imagine their common origin and the meaning of its development. The original stream of consciousness penetrated the substance of thought, organised it so that it slowed down, and separated from its own stream. Some streams of consciousness were waking more and more in the course of development, some of them were falling asleep; the rigidity of some served as the activity of others. Waking up could, according to Bergson, happen in two ways: consciousness penetrating through the substance focused either on its own movement or on the substance which it was organising or penetrating through. It means that life, or to better say, consciousness was oriented towards intuition or intellect (Bergson, 1966).

10.2. Ontology of the Past

Let us stay in Bergson's metaphysics for a while and look more closely at his understanding of memory and matter from which a new conception of ontology results.

This was marked with the term "ontology of the past" by for example Josef Fulka (see: Fulka, J.: Bergson a problém paměti, 2003, p. 30). Bergson rejects the Cartesian views, he affirms the reality of matter and spirit but it does not mean that they exist separately for him. He defines matter as an image: *"Matter, in our view, is an aggregate of `images.'. And by ‚image' we mean a certain existence which is more than that which the idealist calls a representation, but less than that which the realist calls a thing"* (Bergson, 1966) The problem which he is trying to resolve in the treatise Matter and Memory is how the great number of psychological states, which represent the most basic characteristics of our spiritual life, is stored and where it comes from?

Consciousness seems to exceed cerebral activity in all directions. Bergson compares it to a stage behind which many other processes and activities are going on. Even the brain is an image, it creates a part of the material world. The material world cannot exist in the brain, the whole cannot exist in a part (Bergson, Matiére et mémoire, 1936).

Where are memories then stored if it not in the brain or in the CNS in general? According to Bergson, there is a difference between a memory and a current perception which lies in the nature and character. The imperfection of all philosophical conceptions of memory consists of the fact that there was a difference between a memory and a perception only in terms of the intensity. The past was some kind of weak present, emphasis was put on the topicality.

The question **where** the memories are stored is incorrectly put because it mixes temporality and space. The temporality does not dwell in any place, in any space. Distinction of the spirit and matter is of the nature of time and not of space.

When we believe that the past is no more, we mistake "existence" with *"be present."* But the present itself is not; it is rather a clear happening. The present is not but it causes; activity and usefulness are its elements. The very past, useless, inactive, in the true sense of the word, **is**.

Reflections to think about:

Is it possible to approach reality with intuition as was suggested by Bergson? Which weaknesses and imperfections do you see in his conception? What do you think about his relatively controversial thesis that "the past is more ontologically fundamental than the present?"

Recommended literature:

Bergson, H.: Creative Evolution. Courier Corporation, 2012.
Bergson, H.: Matter and Memory. Cosimo, Inc, 2007.
Chevalier, J.: Bergson Henri. New York, The Macmillan Company 1928.

11. Metaphysics and Problem of Being. Martin Heidegger

11.1. The Meaning of Being

Heidegger's philosophical project before the so-called "turn" is based on the search for meaning of being. The question of the meaning of being has, according to him, never been put properly, this ontological question faded into dead obscurity (Heidegger, M.: Being and Time, 2010). If we want to explore being and its meaning we have to use *phenomenology* (see Dreyfus, D.L.: *Being – in-the- world.* Cambridge: MIT Press, 1991, p. 30). However, the early Heidegger always openly committed to phenomenology, he rejected being included in some kind of a movement within phenomenology. By using the phenomenological way of asking a fundamental philosophical question, which means the question of the meaning of being, Heidegger did not, according to himself, acknowledge *"any attitude or movement because phenomenology is nothing like that and it can never be as long as it understands itself"* (Heidegger, 2010).

The expression "phenomenology" itself does not primarily represent anything but a method, which means, the way *how* things are being explored, a way of exploration, of asking questions. He expresses his opinion to a textbook password "to the things themselves" ("zu den Sachen selbst") and this opinion is opposed to all accidental and unfounded constructions, prejudices, habits, seemingly proved theses. The meaning of the programme motto of phenomenology is so natural that if Heidegger wants to move his exploration of being further, he has to firstly fixate (so natural) the term of phenomenology.

The concept of *phenomenology* consists of two words: phenomenon and logos. The etymology of both of them originate in the Greek expressions φαινομενον and λογοσ. The term phenomenology is then formally based on a similar principle as for example biology, theology, anthropology, or in any other life science, God and human. Phenomenology should then analogously be a science about phenomena (Heidegger, 2010). When we look more closely at both components of the term phenomenology, the words *phenomenon* and *logos*, the characteristic and not only formal meaning of these words are uncovered.

11.2. "Phenomenon" as an Expression

The roots of the expression "phenomenon" refer to the Greek verb jainesuai which is translated as "to show itself," to be obvious, clear. φανομενον means then "that which shows itself in itself," "that which is brought to light." *"The meaning of the word phenomenon can be determined as: that which shows itself in itself, that which is obvious"* (Heidegger, 2010). The Greeks probably identified this "obvious" with being. But being can be shown as something which it is not and thus "look like that" or in other words *seeming*. But Heidegger points out that in his understanding (and also in the understanding of phenomenology) the expression *phenomenon* is ascribed with the original positive meaning of the word. Phenomenon is not an illusion.

It cannot be fully identified with occurrence. An occurrence as a manifestation is not "showing itself" but on the contrary, it means that we deal with something that does not show itself using something that shows itself. This complicated pun can be simplified: an occurrence here does not represent that which does not show itself. Heidegger clarifies it by using the example of "the occurrence of a disease." The occurrence of a disease is a set of changes which show themselves, indicate that which does not show itself (Heidegger, 2010). However, the occurrence is never showing itself (in the meaning of the Greek word jainomenon), it is possible only because something shows itself. *"Seeming means to appear by means of that which shows itself"* (Heidegger, 2010). The concept *occurrence* can mean the already mentioned seeming in the meaning of appearing but not showing itself, or – appearing itself – that which by means of its showing itself indicates that which does not show itself. To intensify the terminological chaos, the fourth aspect of the meaning of the word phenomenon is missing and particularly *appearing itself*: *"And finally one can use „appearing" as a term for the genuine sense of „phenomenon" as showing-itself"* (Heidegger, 2010). We can avoid confusion and problems with understanding if from the beginning we understand a phenomenon as that which shows itself in itself. That which is supposed to become a phenomenon is not given from the beginning but it is latent; *latency* functions as a conceptual opposite to phenomenon. The fact that phenomena *are developing* themselves is originally expressed in Aristotle's works, or more particularly, in the entire Greek thinking as alhueia, meaning non-latency of is – being there – as its uncovering, showing-itself (See Heidegger, M.: *Moje cesta k fenomenologii*. In: Heidegger, M.: *Konec filosofie a úkol myšlení*, p. 51).

To clarify the expression phenomenology, there is the second part missing – the clarification of the expression logos.

11.3. "Logos" as an Expression

The word *logos* is in the history of philosophy translated (according to Heidegger always *interpreted* so it is always burdened with some kind of an advanced determined meaning, context or sense) as reason, judgement, concept, definition, ground, and relation (Heidegger, 2010). The basic meaning of the word logos is actually *discourse.* Heidegger justifiably objects to the above mentioned interpretation (or translation). "λογοσ- *as „discourse" means rather the same as dhloun: to make manifest what one is ‚talking about' in one's discourse...the logos- lets something be seen namely, what the discourse is about...discourse ‚let's something be seen'..."* (Heidegger, 2010). For example, Gadamer says that logos, giving speech, revealing things which are in progress has within it something different as the meaning of meanings put into the words and only here *"...the most natural possibility of discourse, namely, communicating something right, true, has its place"* (Gadamer, Truth and Method, 2013).

11.4. Phenomenology

It results from the facts mentioned above concerning the terminological research that the term phenomenology means: *"...to let that which shows itself be seen from itself in the very way in which it shows itself from itself"* (Heidegger, 2010).

Heidegger here actually explains only a known programme dictum "To the things themselves!" Phenomenology proved to be, as for the meaning, a different concept as, for example, theology or biology which determines the subject of the individual disciplines according to the material content. Phenomenology does not characterise its content; it only clarifies *how, in what way* the subject it deals with is handled. The question is with what subject does phenomenology deal with? Or, more precisely, directly from its nature – what is that which phenomenology should allow to be seen, what it should let us see it as it is indeed. This question initially requires evasion – it is obviously a case of the exploration of that which does not show itself at first sight, is *latent.* That which does not at first show itself or shows itself latently as though vaguely and without clear contours is not *that* or *the* being but *existence.* Existence is so latent that is has sunk into oblivion as it is, according to Heidegger, shown by the entire history of philosophy.

Phenomenology is a way of approaching existence where it is necessary to keep in mind Heidegger's radical declaration: *"Only as phenomenology, is ontology possible"* (Heidegger, 2010). Or in other words, phenomenology is as far as its content a science about the existence of being – which means ontology. After the delimitation of the way of exploration and (primarily) and of its subject, we find that Heidegger moves in the field of so-called "fundamental ontology."

The scope of research of Heidegger's fundamental ontology includes the ontological-ontically distinguished being "Dasein," stay, by means of which ontology comes to its most fundamental problem – the question of the meaning of being (Heidegger, 2010). It is important to say that for Heidegger ontology and phenomenology do not represent two different philosophical disciplines; they are not separated by any demarcation line. *"These terms characterize philosophy itself with regard to its object and its way of treating that object. Philosophy is universal phenomenological ontology, and takes its departure from the hermeneutic of Dasein"* (Heidegger, 2010). Three procedures emerged, as for methodology, within Heidegger's approach to being – 1. a transition from a vulgar to a phenomenological phenomenon, in other words, a transition from being to existence that could be defined as *phenomenological reduction,* 2. *hermeneutic anticipation,* or in other words, *phenomenological construction.* It means that phenomenology is here not for itself, but if it wants to be *active* it has to enter the hermeneutic circle of knowledge. It cannot do so without constructive anticipation, from which it results. The phenomenon "to unlock it" can be achieved only by means of working out an adequate pre-understanding. "The Λογοσ has the character of ἑρμηνεέειν through which the authentic meaning of Being, and also those basic structures of Being which Dasein itself possesses, *are made known to Dasein's understanding of Being. The phenomenology of Dasein is hermeneutic in the primordial signification of this word, where it designates this business of interpretin"* (Heidegger, 2010). 3. *Phenomenological destruction* which functions as an imaginary defence against the superficial acceptance of tradition. And since being is for Heidegger an absolutely immanent moment of the above mentioned method, it can be said that ontology and phenomenology are actually one and the same, that they are two interchangeable titles.

11.5. Fundamental Ontology

It was Martin Heidegger who tried to formulate *fundamental ontology* in the twentieth century. His attempt is based on the criticism of western metaphysics which functions as the history of "forgetting of being." According to Heidegger, the old ontology calms itself down by means of establishing the problem of being in order to penetrate into the basic question of being and the meaning of being.

In 1927, Heidegger's treatise *Sein und Zeit* was published where he presented his concept of fundamental ontology. The key topic is the delimitation of philosophy as ontology (which should give a permanent answer to the question of the meaning of being). In the following years (primarily the period of 1928-1929), he emphasises in his philosophy the historicity and the moment. Philosophy moves its influence into the area of worries about the understanding of being which should be grasped authentically; the "unlocking of the world" lies within it. This is one of the shifts that will, in the beginning only imperceptibly, but later very openly cause a deep revolution in his philosophy which he named "die Kehre" (turn, roll).

The question of the meaning of being is, according to Heidegger, heading not only towards a priori condition of the possibility of sciences, which deal with being, but also to the condition of a possibility of ontology itself, which is the base for science. Science is "only" a way of being of Dasein in which it relates to this or that being – but *always* to a being which is fundamentally not Dasein itself. And this is, according to Heidegger, the reason why it is necessary to fill an empty space in the exploration of the existential analytics of Dasein by establishing fundamental ontology.

He insists that being is the most natural and *sole* topic of philosophy (Heidegger, M.: *The basic problems of phenomenology*, p. 11). *"This is not our own invention; it is a way of putting the theme which comes to life at the beginning of philosophy in antiquity, and it assumes its most grandiose form in Hegel's logic"* (Heidegger, M.: *The basic problems of phenomenology,* p. 11). However, he is not convinced that being plays the most natural and singular role in contemporary philosophy. Philosophy stopped being *a science about being*, ontology and was transformed into a science about beings (Heidegger, M.: *The basic problems of phenomenology*, p. 11).

In order to clarify Heidegger's fundamental ontology, it is necessary to explain two aspects which relate to the understanding of being. The first aspect is connected with the definition that being does not seem to be "transparent" at the beginning, as it is itself. Dasein is equipped with a *pre-ontological understanding of being*. *"We have already intimated that Dasein has a pre-ontological Being as its ontically constitutive state"* (Heidegger, 2010). Dasein simply exists in the way that it *understands* being. We could compare it with some kind of taciturn understanding of being of things to which it relates. If we did not understand (at first only roughly and without terms) what reality meant, it would stay concealed from us; if we did not understand what being meant, we could not exist ourselves as Dasein. The same way, if we did not understand what permanency and validity was, mathematical relations would be unclear to us.

We as Dasein have to understand reality, being, permanency so that we can relate to them in a positive way. This preontological understanding of being would be delimited and interpreted in two ways. Firstly, it can be connected with the undifferentiated understanding of being in the history of philosophy and here being seems to be relatively differentiated. After all, Dasein in everyday actions takes into consideration ontological differences: it treats people differently from animals, animals differently from plants, plants differently from mathematical relationships. The second way is Heidegger's own – it means that if we connect the preontological understanding of being with Heidegger's understanding of being, the result will be that our everyday understanding of being is rough, veiled, without concepts, vague, and undifferentiated.

Despite that it functions as a great base, "a springboard" for the next achievements: *"But in that case the question of Being is nothing other than the radicalization of an essential tendency-of-Being which belongs to Dasein itself – the pre-ontological understanding of Being"* (Heidegger, 2010). The second aspect is connected with the relationship between the terms *understanding of being* and *transcendental*. Heidegger's fundamental ontology is, like hermeneutics of transcendence, transcendental philosophy and, moreover, this ontology perceives the understanding of being as a primary form of understanding as such. If we take into account a hermeneutical circle of understanding, we have no choice but to agree with Heidegger – the more perfect our pre-understanding of being is, the less veiled being seems to be. It is a paradox that Dasein is somehow aware of diversity of being but, in spite of it, usually has only a vague idea of being; a specific way of being of e.g. animals, plants, mathematical-geometric relations is known to us but this known is unknown as such (Heidegger, Kant and The Problem of Metaphysics, 1997). Heidegger clarifies this paradox in his fundamental ontological conception by means of existential structure of Dasein and its tendency to unauthenticity and decline. Dasein allows the world to absorb it in a busy way, lazily, curiously and in a hurry which leads to an undifferentiated concept of being. This is controlled by the existence of those things which impose themselves on Dasein in its everydayness (it is a case of so-called "occurring existences"). Dasein is then groping around the understanding of its own being that Heidegger defines with the expression "ontological reflection" – an interpretation of Dasein is retroactively influenced by the understanding of the world. It is necessary to keep in mind that it is not a case of some kind of moralising awakening of authenticity, to takeover of "reins" of its being but on the contrary – Heidegger wants to fundamentally ontologically clarify the origin of the veiled and average understating of being.

This aspect also has a historical context. If fundamental ontology should deal with being, it has to consult it with the up-to-now historical-philosophical questions about being. It was already mentioned that Heidegger concluded that understanding of history was veiled, prejudiced and deformed and he is therefore trying to take a turn for movement as an opposite to it: *"If, then, the answer to the question of Being is to provide the clues for our research, it cannot be adequate until it brings us the insight that the specific kind of Being of ontology hitherto, and the vicissitudes of its inquiries, its findings, and its failures, have been necessitated in the very character of Dasein"* (Heidegger, 2010). The orientation of traditional ontology lies in the *blurriness* which results from its focus on the inner-worldly being, but as for the relationship of Dasein to the inner-worldly existences, the philosophical tradition is authorised to criticise as it does not take into consideration a practical approach. Only a theoretical approach has ever been comforting for those in which existence occurred only incidentally. Heidegger introduced a differentiation between the different subjects of exploration and searching between the determining (leading) and the basic exploration of philosophy. The leading position has belonged to metaphysics since the Middle Ages with the question "what is existence as such?" In Heidegger's fundamental ontology this is overcome by the question "what is the meaning of being?" This is a *basic* question. We do not ask "what is existence as existence?" but "what is being?" Heidegger managed to differentiate the asking itself from the classic ontological tradition. Not only that, Heidegger and his project showed that *the basic asking* presupposes *the leading asking* which is implicitly incorporated in it and thus *overcome.*

Ontology and metaphysics should have been, from the point of view of the project, brought back to basics. We intentionally mention metaphysics alongside ontology since the fundamental ontology of the early Heidegger from *Being and Time* can be understood as thinking within metaphysics although some objections can be found to metaphysics connected with the forgetting of being. *"Metaphysics speaks of what be-ing is as be-ing; it offers a λόγος (statement) about ón (be-in). The later term „ontology" indicates its essence, supposing, that is, that we interpret the term according to its own proper content and not in a narrow scholastic sense. Metaphysics moves in the realm of ón h ón. Its formulating concerns be-ing as be-ing. In this way, metaphysics always formulates be-ing as such as a whole as the be-ingness of be-ing"* (Heidegger, M.: *Úvod k přednášce "Co je metafyzika?"* In: HEIDEGGER, M.: *Co je metafysika?*, p. 31).

11.6. Problem of Metaphysics after the "Turn"

Metaphysics, as long as it imagines existence as existence, is not the being itself and philosophy this way moves away from its fundamental base *through* metaphysics itself. Heidegger's later philosophy is not content with metaphysics but he not against metaphysics either. *"Figuratively speaking, it does not „uproot" the root of philosophy; it digs into its ground and ploughs its land"* (Heidegger, 2006). However, metaphysics continues to be firstly philosophy, it does not reach what are the first thoughts, which means the truth of being. Metaphysics here is a thing of the past. It is necessary to take into account that Heidegger does not want to get rid of metaphysics by this relatively radical statement. *"As long as man is the animal rationale, he is the animal metaphysicum"* (Heidegger, 2006). Getting over *die Verwindung* (Heidegger preferred the term die Verwindung to the word die Überwindung with which he manifested that he does not want to "fight" with metaphysics. Die Überwindung means defeating, overcoming) of metaphysics does not mean here an anti-metaphysical approach but an effort to get to being by means of the return into the rudiments of metaphysics. The question inevitably arises why Heidegger needed to overcome metaphysics? Do the roots of philosophy need to be replaced by something more original, "reconstructed" philosophy? No. He is rather trying to get to the original being with a step back from metaphysics into the beingness of metaphysics. Before metaphysics started to deal with the question of existence as such, it was interested in being. *"But now metaphysics continually and in the most various ways speaks about being"* (Heidegger, 2006). In the meantime, metaphysics harbours throughout its history from Anaximander to Nietzsche. It never answered the question about the truth of being because it never asked it. Metaphysics confuses the whole existence with being (Heidegger, 2006). Heidegger does not see it as a mistake of negligence but of superficial expression. Metaphysics should be based on what is hidden in existence but it does not deal with existence as existence. Questions aimed at what is hidden in existence is, according to Heidegger, looking for a fundamental of ontology. This is the reason why he named his procedure in Being and Time the fundamental ontology (Heidegger, 2006). When he deals with it again after the "turn" in a lecture *Einleitung zu: "Was ist Metaphysik?"*, he claims that fundamental ontology is a misleading name. It is correct from the metaphysical point of view but this is what leads, according to Heidegger, to chaos because the idea is to get from metaphysics to thoughts of the truth of being. If he insisted on the name fundamental ontology even after the "turn," he would, in his own words, make it more non-transparent and obscured (Heidegger, 2006). *"Of course, the term „fundamental ontology" suggests the view that thinking which attempts to think the truth of being and not, like all ontology, the truth of be-ing, is even as fundamental ontology still a kind of ontology. Meanwhile, thinking of the truth of being as getting to the bottom of metaphysics has with the first step it takes already abandoned the sphere of all ontology. By comparison, all philosophy that turns on a straightforward or indirect formulation of „transcendence" necessarily remains ontology in an essential sense, whether it wants to effect the laying of the foundations of metaphysics or to assure us that it rejects ontology as a conceptual freezing of living"* (Heidegger, 2006).

Heidegger moved from the term fundamental ontology and the overcoming of metaphysics to the question "what is philosophy" although it can be said that this question is a constant one in his philosophical projects, more or less, implicitly or explicitly still present in his works (in a compact and expanded way I deal with the topic of Heidegger's understanding of fundamental ontology and philosophy in an article: *Filozofia ako fundamentálna ontológia. Čím je filozofia podľa Heideggera?* In: Cestami Heideggerovho myslenia, pp. 220-236).

Reflections to think about:

Try to find in literature other understandings of phenomenology than Heidegger's. Compare the understanding of metaphysics according to Aristotle and according to Heidegger. What would be, in your opinion, Heidegger's reaction to the idea of metaphysics in the individual conceptions which were discussed in this work?

Recommended literature:

Dreyfus, D.L.: Being – in-the- world. Cambridge: MIT Press, 1991.
Heidegger, M.: Being and Time. Suny Press, 2010.
Heidegger, M.: The basic problems of phenomenology. Bloomington: Indiana University Press, 1988.

Conclusion

This university textbook dealt with the individual problems concerning the history of metaphysics and ontology. Of course, this topic has not been fully covered. There was no space left for an analysis of Aristotelian hylemorphism and its subsequent completion in the works of Thomas Aquinas. Another attractive topic, which unfortunately was not given space in this university textbook, would also be existence and its understanding according to K. Jaspers, J.P. Sartre or A. Camus. There are plenty of problems and concepts which were not discussed so let them be "a thrown down gauntlet" for the reader to study them using the recommended literature. The text is supposed to function as a guideline for orientation in the topic and literature which deal with the particular authors and questions. In closing, there is a list of chosen recommended literature concerning the systematic and historical point of view of metaphysics:

Systematic point of view

Burkhardt, H., Smith, B.: *Handbook of Metaphysics and Ontology, I-II*, 1991, Analytica Philosophia Verlag, Mníchov.
Hamlyn, D.W.: Metaphysics, 1984, Cambridge University Press.
Hasker, W.: Metaphysics, InterVarsity Press, 1983.
Inwagen van P.: Ontology, Identity and Modality: Essays in Metaphysics, Cambridge University Press, 2001.
Loux, M.J.: Metaphysics: A Contemporary Introduction, Psychology Press, 2002.
Poli, R., Seibt, J.: Theory and Applications of Ontology: Philosophical Perspectives, Springer Science & Business Media, 2010.
Strawson, P.F.: Individuals. An Essay in Descriptive Metaphysics, London, 1959.
Strawson, P.F.: Analysis and Metaphysics. An Introduction to Philosophy, Oxford, 1992.

Historical point of view:

Doig, J.C.: Aqinas on Metaphysics, Den Haag, 1972.
Grondin, J.: Introduction to Metaphysics: From Parmenides to Levinas, Columbia University Press, 2013.
Heidegger, M.: The Fundamental Concepts of Metaphysics: World, FInitude, Solitude, Indiana University Press, 2001.
Krapiec, M.A.: Metaphysics: An Outline of the History of Being, P. Lang, 1991.
Moore, A.W.: The Evolution of Modern Metaphysics: Making Sense of Things, Cambridge University Press, 2012.

Bibliography

Anselm, Wiliams, T.: Proslogion: With the Replies of Gaunilo and Anselm, 2001, Hacket Publishing.
Aristetle: The Organon. Nabu Press, 2011
Aristotle: Metaphysics, University of Michigan, 1978.
Bergson, H.: La pensée et le mouvant. Paris, Les Presses universitaires de France 1969.
Bergson, H.: Matiére et mémoire. Paris, Les Presses universitaires de France, 1936.
Bergson, H.: L'évolution créatrice. Paris, Presses universitaires de France 1966.
Carr, B.: Metaphysics: An Introduction. Humanities Press International, 1987.
Deleuze, G.: Bergsonismus. Praha, Garamond 2006.
de Libera, A.: Středověká filosofie. Praha: OIKOYMENH, 2001.
Dionysios Areopagita: Listy. O mystické theologii. Praha: OIKOYMENH, 2005.
Dionysios Areopagita: O mystické teologii. O Božských jménech. Praha: Dybbuk, 2003.
Dreyfus, D.L.: Being – in-the- world. Cambridge: MIT Press, 1991.
Eliade, M.: The Myth of the Eternal Return: Cosmos and History. Princeton University Press, 2012.

Gadamer, H.G.: Truth and Method. Bloomsbury Academic, 2013
Heidegger, M.: Being and Time, State University of New York Press, 2010
Heidegger, M.: Kant and the Problem of Metaphysics, Indiana University Press, 2004.
Heidegger, M.: Moje cesta k fenomenologii. In: HEIDEGGER, M.: Konec filosofie a úkol myšlení. Praha: OIKOYMENH, 2006.
Heidegger, M.: The basic problems of phenomenology. Bloomington: Indiana University Press, 1988.
Heidegger, M.: Úvod k přednášce „Co je metafyzika?" In: HEIDEGGER, M.: Co je metafysika? Praha: OIKOYMENH, 2006.
Hrdlička, J.: O intuici u Bergsona. In: Filosofie Henri Bergsona. Praha, OIKOYMENH 2003.
http://plato.stanford.edu/entries/metaphysics/
http://plato.stanford.edu/entries/universals-medieval
Hume, D.: An Enquiry Concerning Human Understanding. Oxford University Press, 2007.
Chevalier, J.: Bergson Henri. New York, The Macmillan Company 1928.
James W.: Pragmatism, Harvard University Press, 1975.
Kant, I.: The Critique of Pure Reason, Start Publishing LLC, 2012.
Kišoňová, R.: Filozofia ako fundamentálna ontológia. Čím je filozofia podľa Heideggera? In: Cestami Heideggerovho myslenia, s. 220-236.
Kouba, P.: Pohyb medzi časem a prostorem. In: Filosofie Henri Bergsona. Praha, OIKOYMENH 2003.
Koudelka, M.: Nauka o pozitivní a negativní theologii v Dionysiových Listech a Mystické theologii. In: DIONYSIOS AREOPAGITA: Listy. O mystické theologii. Praha: OIKOYMENH, 2005.
Lactanius: Divine Institutes: Bks. 1-7 (Fathers of the Church Series). Washington: The Catholic University of America Press, 1992.
Le Goff, J.: Time, Work and Culture in the Middle Ages. The University of Chicago Press, 1982.
Lemon, M.C.: Philosophy of History, London: Routledge, 2003.
Markoš, A.: Přírodní zákony a evoluce. In: Filosofie Henri Bergsona. Praha, OIKOYMENH 2003.
Nietzsche, F.: Thus Spoke Zarathustra. Oxford University Press, 2005.
Owens, J.: Saint Thomas Aquinas on the Existence of God: The Collected Papers of Joseph Owens, 1980, Sunny Press.
Peregrin, J.: Filosofie pro normální lidi. Praha: Dokořán. 2008.

Porubjak, M.: Vôľa (k) celku. Človek a spoločenstvo rečou Homéra a Theognida. Pusté Úľany: Schola Philosophica, 2010.
Proslogion, in: Sokol J.: Mistr Eckhart a středověká mystika, Praha, 1993.
Quine, V.W.: Pursuit of Truth, Harvard University Press, 1990.
Sandywell, B.: The Beginnings of European Theorizing – reflexivity in the Archaic Age, Psychology Press, 1996.
Schmidinger, W.: Metaphysik: Ein Grundkurs. Kohlhammer, 2010.
Sýkora, P.: Ontológia šera, Pusté Úľany: Schola Philosophica, 2008.
The Routledge Companion to Metaphysics, Routledge, 2009.
W.O.Döring: Das Lebenswerk Immanuel Kants, 1947, Hamburg.
Walsh, M.J.: A history of Philosophy. London , 1985
Welsch, W.: Unsere postmoderne Moderne, Walter de Gruyter, 2008.

Renáta Kišoňová studied Philosophy at the University of Trnava. Her research interests include the problems of metaphysics.